D1527623

A FLAME
FOR THE
TOUCH
THAT
MATTERS

Books by Michael Lassell

Poems for Lost and Un-lost Boys (Amelia, 1985)
Decade Dance (Alyson, 1990)
The Hard Way (A Richard Kasak Book, 1995)

Books edited by Michael Lassell

The Name of Love: Classic Gay Love Poems
(St. Martin's Press, 1995)
Eros in Boystown: Contemporary Gay Poems About Sex
(Crown Publishers, 1996)

with Lawrence Schimel
Two Hearts Delight: Gay Couples on Their Love
(St. Martin's Press, 1997)

MICHAEL LASSELL

For dear Amir K.

A Flame
for the
Touch That
Matters

Much love, and many Thanks

Poems

for your friendship and support.

Michael Lassell

Painted Leaf Press
New York City

Cover design by James Maszle
Text design by Brian Brunius

Library of Congress Cataloging-in-Publication Data

Lassell, Michael, 1947-
    A flame for the touch that matters: poems / Michael Lassell
        p.   cm.
    ISBN 0-9651558-9-7
    I. Title
    PS3562.A7527F57   1998
    811'.54--dc21
                                                97-41686
                                                     CIP

For Michael Angel Nava

Contents

Four

Five

One

Kissing Ramón

One kisses Ramón good-night on Bank Street in the Village.

At the corner, the bank is expanding into the bookstore, and Ramón tells you about the poet laureate of the Philippines, who lives down the street, on Greenwich.

Sometimes the kisses are long and deep, and there are passersby.

Sometimes one grows hard almost instantly.

"Shut off your fucking engine," the policewoman bellows through her bullhorn.

Bullets.

Sirens.

Sometimes his ear is ice on one's flushed cheek.

A fat man in a tight jacket turns the lights of his van on from a block away.

Masculine Principle No. 1 (Urban)
All men must own a car. All cars must have alarm systems. All alarm systems must make intrusive electronic noises whenever activated or deactivated, no matter how obnoxious this may be to one who is trying to cheat the dark of its tariff (insomnia) by falling asleep before midnight realizes what's happened.

Masculine Principle No. 1 (Rural)
Insert the words "pick-up truck" for the word "car" above.

Masculine Principle No. 2
One kisses Ramón and wonders about the moisture that lingers on one's lips and in one's mustache, despite all pub-

lished evidence that kissing, even deep wet slopping kissing, is relatively safe. But what is safety in this day and age?

One wipes away the saliva, feels guilty, brushes one's teeth, feels guilty, masturbates, feels unfulfilled, falls to sleep, is wakened by:

Men's voices: angry shouting.
Women's voices: hurt, weeping.

Intrusive electronic noises.

Mice running in the wall; rats warring in the walls.

Screaming in feminine French.
Screaming in masculine Spanish.

"Shut off your fucking engine," the policewoman bellows
  through her bullhorn.

You think you'd like to swallow bullets: soft, sweet, deadly.

Sometimes one touches Ramón's ass just for luck, like
  Buddha's belly.

Masculine Principle No. 3
Ramón buys baklava at a deli on Ninth Avenue. One waits with Ramón in the cold for the Abingdon Square bus. One mentions the death of a mutual friend. Ramón explains his life on Planet Positive, his fear of death, his anger and denial. Speechless with grief and without experience, one still feels a need to respond.

Sometimes one feels Ramón's cheek and it's as soft as sifted
  flour.

Kisses.

Bullets.

Sirens.

At home

That Saturday the Federal Express
from Orlando never came, probably
because of the nor'easter that twisted
through New York from midnight snow to a slush-
splattered dawn. There wasn't anything in
the box, anyway, just a heavy load
I didn't feel like hauling home after
a business trip that wasted precious time.

Besides, I was being haunted by my
memories: of overzealous sex with
Jorge—*who's not*, he repeats, a whore—and
of tooth-tugging his new nipple ring while
he finger-fucked the shit out of me, which
reminds me how tenderness dropped out of
my life when age crept in on silent crow's
feet (he charged a hundred and twenty bucks);

of Ron, the editor of that teener
hip-hop rag, the last man I had sex with
free, who had me to his darkened room when
we were both in Florida before, whose
ass and model's mouth were most receptive,
but this time averted his eyes, his back
literally turned, as if I were a
beggar with a cup in my taloned claw;

of the glow the midnight shuttle launch from
nearby Cape Canaveral left in the
artificial lake, as we watched from a
roof; how vast the notion of "space" seemed as
the booster rockets fell, the merest twin
red specks plunging backward into the dark
empty sea—like the sinking feeling I
get as I drop off to sleep every night;

of how unlike life "alone" feels, how far
away the infinite. I forgave Ron
in that incendiary moment on
top of the Contemporary Resort.
By Saturday, I was weary. Hunger
and lust slept in—but not longing, that tear-
stalker in deerskin, as alive as the
'Sixties on Nickelodeon TV.

Blond mendacity

His name was... I forget (unusual
for me). It was, I recall, just slightly
off-normal—Kirk? In any event an
obvious *nom de guerre* for his nightly
ads in local newspaper personals.

He looks voluptuous in camouflage
fatigues and worn boots. Approving, he scans
the plantation decor and then strips—slow,
indolent as old hotel ceiling fans.
(Bottle blond, he well exceeds "twenty-two.")

He was... adequate—bloated around the
waist, and not really versatile in bed
(as promised). Hopeless as a bottom, well
enough hung, he gives salubrious head.
Not even a cock ring keeps him hard long.

He groans with (feigned?) satisfaction, jerking
nearly off but doesn't come (I surmise
I am not his last). His mouth, lubricious
with cash, is no ruse—a scalding surprise
to us both. After I geyser, he grins.

In the steaming shower he lathers me
up, kisses so sweetly, I touch his thigh
scar. He was into leather in his teens,
he explains, but I hope it's a bald lie—
a perjury to mask his certain bruise.

Uptown local

Fine hair in long unplaited
tendrils, a Flemish painting but
wet black, someone Dürer might have

etched.

Black shoes and shorts, white
socks and shirt. Skin with history
in its pigment and equatorial

attitude.

Seated, knees together like a girl.
It is the fuller upper lip that
makes his mouth seem carved,

totemic.

He looks up, beatific, directly
into my unsated gaze, without
haste, hesitation, or altered

aspect.

An insect, frightened by noise,
scuttles below the bench he
sits on, his book a study of

Bauhaus.

Aboard, I scribble. He rests his
eyes, opens heavy lids once, to
smile at a youngster's insistent

simplicity.

At Times Square, we get off, single
file. He is yards ahead in the
heat. Even his easy speed is

charged.

Slowly, he merges with the crowd,
a mystical boy who appears, then
slips into the hungry urban

ether.

Stroke of midnight

Love after dark is a complex
illusion: lunacy or lust,
a simple discharge of the
day's disappointments,
a certain nostalgia for
bathhouse abandon,
miscellaneous need.

Midnight is often mistaken.

Brazilian boy of
twenty-two,
slim-hipped boy
who studies ballet and
strips in a Times Square
dive between clients:

In the wee hours—
my hands tied to your hair,
my rubber-coated cock
working inside you—I
call this intercourse of
commerce forever diamonds
and know it's as real as
the scar on your belly,
the money you crave
on your tongue.

Bathhouse/Burma/Winston
and the perfection of a strawberry

Nights at the baths, I make love to a Burmese boy/man who lives in the suburbs. His name is Leon, he tells me, as I place one hand on him and tell him mine. His nipples—russet petals of an autumn in miniature—harden after brief attention. We spread white towels on the top shelf of the hot room and fall to hard tongues/soft hands/eyelids. I lean back on wet tiles, hold his hair in steaming fists. I see out the window: swimming pool, freeway, stars. Sweat pours off us, glitters like lamplight on the headdresses of the temple dancers. In the shower, in the coagulation of moment to memory, he tells me, oh yes, he has heard of my city and feigns interest in its dimension.

Later, I catch in the corner of my eye: Winston, a memory in profile, four years of pony tail pulled off his moon face. Ten years ago, I'd have killed for the tangerine musk of his curls. Chinese, he was, and loved, I called it, Gavin of the mane and torso, poems and sorrow, big ideas and flower-sack pantaloons. (Winston and Gavin go at each other in the back of a van on the I-5; their lovemaking rises in my ears like the perfection of a strawberry at the mere mention of either name.) Eight years ago, I cut him off on Roberto's say-so and have missed him ever since. Now, at half-past two in the old a.m., there is Winston in his clothes checking out of the baths. He does not see me. I do not speak. Once I felt his every gesture in my thigh; now I still do not know if it was really him—Winston of the puppets, masks, and scones (and Gavin in my head again as he was at eighteen).

Later, sitting in my car in front of the Mexican tenement, it occurs to me to crave: strawberries picked in summer and boiled down to jam, strawberry wine and margaritas, tortes and tarts and cold parfait, Strawberry Alarm Cock and Fields Forever and Gavin. Had not Rose become rose earlier in the century, he could be a rose, but now he is a strawberry, and I want 'im—bad.

I pull the choke, turn the ignition. The engine warms.

Dancer(s) with Dick(s)
at the 1 Saloon, Key West

I have one hand on his cock, the other
deeply involved with the shaven every-
thing between his balls and asshole, at which

willing target I've aimed my spit-slick thumb.
"All *right*," he says, bending to help me and
offer a kiss, "work *me!*" I don't want to

disappoint, so I pop one proffered tit
in my mouth while he grinds that totally
tubular rod of his into my palm.

"My name is Chris," he says. He's a solo
tonight (the other dancer's father had
a stroke). "You are a hot daddy," he says,

which takes me aback (I feel twenty-six
most of the time). I give him another
buck: "I guess I'm getting there," I shuffle.

"No getting there involved," he says, his brown
forehead a furrow, "you have *arrived*." I
take him at his word—after all, he's the

pro. He might just be right. So, now I'm a
daddy, I think and let it sink slowly
in. Well, it's better than nothing, I guess—

here at the far end of further away
than anywhere and way beyond what the
hell. You know what I mean, pretty baby?

Personal foibles #2

Just because I like feet
doesn't mean I'm a fetishist.
I admit to a certain
fascination, not adulation
but certainly not revulsion
either. Women's shoes hold me
like a moth flame. I could have
sucked the tiny toes of
the Sikh waiter in Delhi all
night long instead of just
four hours;
and then there was this
sweet hustler in San
Francisco who charged by the
shiatsu massage and groaned with
pleasure not the first time I
put his dick in my mouth but
the first time I touched his soles,
his cowboy boots erect at bedside.
I wanted to squeeze those balls
and knead those heels until
my brother of mercy was
helpless with rapture, to
work my knuckles into the wrinkled
flesh of his feet until he dropped
in mindless abandon. And of all the
things to notice about the
nude hunk on the runway, I
was swept away by the pedicured
perfection of his toes—
the nails trimmed on
a diamond template. And
why of all the things
that must have been said at a
party twenty years ago
do I remember only: "His feet
were beautiful. They were the feet
of a sculptor's model"?

That boy on the pier

I want to kiss that boy on the pier, but
he stares at the olive river, peacock
sky—anywhere but in my direction.
(He is angling for fresher game than me.)
Below us, inch-long fish, invisible
except for enormous eyes, swim upstream
and leap each drifting stick in sport, it seems—
or is it desperation multiplied
by years pursuing the baited prize? And
what's that floating by—that bag of pale gray
bloat? The gas-filled torso of a poet
past his prime, perhaps, who wanted to kiss
a boy's sweet lips one last time, but fell in
love with a river that did not say no?

Two

SCAB, THE TEETH and TONGUES

Scab's lament

Dig me a poem to hide myself in
when teeth scream and
tongues poke through smiles.

A poem is louder than dreams.

The Teeth is huge: He fills the
hall, roaring forward as if
on wheels to devour, devour.

Think of triangles, sharpened.

Tongues is quiet in her rage
and clings to walls like
cotton, swollen and bloody.

In her circles: lies, lies.

Dig me a poem to bury me in
and line it with satin
to soothe the blistered skin.

And in my hexagon: silence.

Hospitality

Tongues goes to the hospital with a
baby inside her and comes back empty.

And alone.

Scab rushes to greet her, but she is
nursing a hollow that becomes a need.

Hush!

Nobody tells him where his brother has gone,
but Scab knows she's killed him for not being perfect.

The Teeth never talks again.

And Tongues never sleeps.

The Silence happens.

Hush!

Scab thinks if he is perfect she will love him.

He never stops eating.

Scab's *TV Guide*

He remembers Howdy Doody and Buffalo Bob.
Princess Summer Fall kept getting killed
in crashes and being replaced. Clarabell
became Cap'n Kangaroo right after Miss
Frances, and The Teeth actually knew him
(the Merry Mailman, too) but never said so.

He remembers watching *The Lone Ranger* one
Saturday noon with Tongues and The Teeth
in front of the mahogany console he wasn't
allowed to touch (it smelled of cedar, paste wax,
and Ella Fitzgerald 78s). Tonto kneeled and
cradled the wounded kemo sabe in his arms.

Lassie always came to the rescue and so
did Rin Tin Tin. Scab never had a dog, and
when Trigger died he was stuffed by Roy
and Dale. He got a parakeet instead called
Happy, but it wasn't. It kept flying into
the mirror and getting stuck behind the TV.

Loretta Young's husband was always killed
in Korea. Gertrude Berg was someone's mom,
and there was a flood. She was afraid of
the safety line, but she finally got on it.
It snapped; she was swept away in the file
footage. Scab got hysterical and went to bed.

They watched Ed Sullivan, but The Teeth and
Tongues talked all the way through it. Tongues was
in love with Perry Como and sang along
to the tunes she knew. The Teeth liked crime
stories and long, boring things that turned
out to be the McCarthy hearings and wars.

There was a drama in black and white. A man and woman were fighting in their car, then stopped at a café. The woman went to the bathroom and vanished into thin air. The man was distraught, the mystery never solved. Scab never let Tongues out of his sight again.

In The Teeth's old Dodge

The Teeth drives a '48 Dodge.
Scab rides in the back alone.
In his dreams, the Dodge begins to roll—
backward down a hill,
but The Teeth is gone.

Scab is alone in the back seat of the car,
his child's pink cheek scratched by gray mohair.

The fear is beating in his heart, but after a dozen
times, he knows it's only a dream
and tells himself he can stop it by
jamming his fingers
into his eyes.

A Dodge that smells of unfiltered Camels.

Just push your fingers into your eyes, he tells
himself in the dreams.

In the other dream, The Teeth is also absent.
An atom blast sends a
mushroom cloud up over the city.

Scab squats behind the fire hydrant near the
mailbox waiting for The Teeth to come.

He knows The Teeth will come because
The Teeth is a fireman. And when he comes
everything will be fine.

He squats there.
Waiting.

Tongues' vocabulary lesson

You live in a world of your own.
Your head is in the clouds.

Over my dead body.

No.

You're lazy/selfish/
irresponsible/
ungrateful/weird.

I'll give you something to cry about.

No.

Nothing is ever enough for you.
Nothing is ever good enough.

You never finish anything/
never follow through.
If you can't do something right away, you just give up.

You'll be sorry when we're dead.
Don't be such a crybaby!

No.

If he gets any fatter I don't know what we'll do.
No one will ever love you like your mother.
Where do you get these crazy ideas?
You're not wearing that.
I'll forgive, but I'll never forget.
There's nothing wrong.

You just say these things to upset me.

No.

Your father is the most handsome man in the world.
You don't look anything like him.

If I wasn't here you'd be helpless.
You're out of your mind.
You want your cake and want to eat it, too.

You don't even mean that.

You read too much/
think too much.
You're too sensitive.

No.

It isn't normal.
No son of mine.
Don't be ridiculous.

You're a great disappointment.

I told you so.

Don't you talk to me that way.
Don't ever say that word.
Don't ever use that tone.
Don't even think about it.

I'm embarrassed and ashamed.

No one cares what you think.
You have no right to express an opinion.
You have no right to have an opinion.

Just who do you think you are?

Who do you think you are?

The Teeth's anger

The Teeth's anger digs its knees into Scab's chest.

The Teeth's anger pounds its meaty fists all over his face.

The Teeth's anger pokes into his ears like nail files, sharpened.

The Teeth's anger cuts into his throat like soldering wire.

The Teeth's anger holds Scab upside down by the ankles.

The Teeth's anger stings his legs like leather and aftershave.

The Teeth's anger seeps from his dark eyes like saliva.

The Teeth's anger squeezes Scab's lungs like boa constrictors.

The Teeth's anger lunges after Scab like a Doberman, leashless.

The Teeth's anger chases him upstairs like a posse.

The Teeth's anger corners him by the bed like a jackal.

The Teeth's anger pins Scab to the floor like steel spikes.

The Teeth's crusading anger flays him like an infidel.

The Teeth's enormous fury is deaf but is not mute or blind.

Patchwork Tongues

Tongues was a red velvet curtain
Scab slept in nine months—nearly
ten: eleven pounds at birth.

Tongues was a cotton housedress
printed with ivy. Scab was the
starch in her pleated ruffle.

Tongues was a clean sheet he sat
under while she ironed and sang
"The Tennessee Waltz." He wooed her.

She was a linen handkerchief and
he an embroidered cherry to keep
her from sickness and sadness.

At night she was lace over satin,
a glimmer of diamonds, the scent
of French perfume on her neck.

In bed she was gossamer trimmed
in silk, the bedclothes whispered
beneath their constant never-touching.

Why Scab hates his teeth

The Teeth speaks:

The dentist says you need braces on your teeth, but he says it's not because there's anything wrong with your bite, that it's only cosmetic, but he can straighten your teeth if you want, but it will cost a lot of money, and I don't know where the hell we would get it, but if you really, really, want to have your teeth straightened, we'll find the money somewhere, though God knows where, and, besides, straight teeth are for girls, why would a boy need straight teeth?—that's what I don't understand, not to mention how painful they are. So, tell me: Do you still want braces?

Scab says no, of course.

The Teeth buys a new car.

Scab sets fire to the shopping center.

Why Scab is drowning

1.
Scab is paddling around naked in the junior high school pool.
He is the only boy who is naked.

Scab is naked because the school does not have a
bathing suit big enough to fit him.

(His fat ass.)

The Teeth says he should be grateful to have a pool to be
   naked in.

The school will not let Scab bring a bathing suit from home.

Tongues says she is sure they know what they are doing.

Danny Rosencheeks points at Scab's dick and howls:
That's the smallest dick I've ever seen. You don't even have
   one!

Scab stays in the shallow end and pretends he can't swim.

2.
In the afternoon, Scab is trying to figure out Homer:
Why is Odysseus trying to go home?

But The Teeth finds him reading and bellows:
Get off your fat ass and go mow the lawn!

The doctor says I'm allergic to grass, Scab says,
the panic rising,
rising.

Just shut your mouth and do what I say.
I don't want to hear any of your lip!

And he doesn't want to be beaten, so he mows
the lawn and then goes to bed for a week.

Tongues pays Scab a midnight visit

At first the dream is harmless enough:
A dolly shot down the streets of Brooklyn,
the home Scab knew as a toddler
and still sees from time to time en route to JFK.

The miracle of sleep:
He is three years old again.
The stairway from the pickle shop to the railroad flat is
painted white, an enamel bathed in celestial light;
workmen in white overalls repair the antique metal stair
(a lace of disintegration).

In the green kitchen, he remembers, Aunt Saintly
cooked his dinner when he ran to her safety.

Then Tongues comes in (silhouetted).

1.   She puts a blanket over his head
     (thick, wool, camphorous).
2.   You're burning up, she says,
     as if he needs her after all these years.
3.   She hoists her nightgown and strides his
     three-year-old hips, pulls it over the auburn
     nimbus of her aureate hair.
               *(Her breasts are a young woman's breasts
               from an imagined memory of nursing.)*
4.   She asks him, begs him, Put your
     fingers in me, grinds down onto him,
     suffocating, pulls his fingers toward her.

I'm already dripping, she says,
and Scab wakes up gasping,
gasping.

But Aunt Saintly's kitchen wasn't green, he thinks,
then dresses for work.

Baseball

The Teeth was a Giants fan when they were in New York.

Scab was a Brooklyn Dodger.

He joined the Little League one Memorial Day and marched
in a parade, his uniform too hot and too tight. He never played.

Then both teams moved and they tore down the stadiums.
Mr. Lasagna took him to see the Yankees (but it didn't factor).

Later Scab moved to California, and The Teeth stayed put.

Mr. Lasagna hanged himself in his neighbor's garage.

Scab went to see the Los Angeles Dodgers with a photographer
friend and ate hot dogs while the men and their sons cheered.

When the Giants appeared on TV the day of the earthquake,
Scab wept because a boy he loved in San Francisco had died.

Scab's back in New York City. They're Mets fans, now, The
    Teeth and
Scab. Actually Scab doesn't give a shit. And the Teeth is losing
    interest.

Scab does have a black leather baseball on his bookshelf.
But it's never been thrown.

At heart The Teeth is still a Giant.

Scab is still a Dodger.

Three

How to go to the art museum

It will be the 44th anniversary of Pearl Harbor,
when kamikazes rose from the sun and sank
the Yank fleet in Hawaii without warning.

Your lover will be out of town for the
second weekend in a row; your car will be stalled
by the side of a road, its battery dead as
your bankbook, the turtle you
dropped on its shell at twelve and cried.

At noon the exterminators arrive uninvited to
ransack your closets with cockroach dust.
You are ordered to vacate the property a minimum of
four hours. You will comply, but
you will hate them silently, swearing as you go, so
dispossessed a citizen.

Driving Ben's Nova feels like a fever,
like swelling glands, swimming in a strange sea.

*　*　*

You are in love with an 18th-century Etonian.
Sir Thomas Lawrence must have loved him, too
(despite his affair with the outcast queen). You
stand in awe of his beauty and youth.
His hair is long,
the unchained male, the boys who
were yours for awhile in unheated cabins by
frozen lakes, who kissed away snowflakes under
birch trees and wallowed in the wisdom of idleness—
who grew into men with
bad memories and wives.

Poor Claude Monet is off the walls today;
Degas and Renoir went with him. Two guards lean
in the empty room; neither has a
clue of humor. You need
miraculous healing, but
Singer Sargent's devil-red doctor is
out on loan in-
definitely,
the man (or boy) wearing laurels
put in permanent storage to teach him a lesson in
perversity.

*   *   *

Yoshi hanged himself from the roof beams.
His mother flew in from
Tokyo for a Buddhist funeral in a blue-gabled
temple on Second Street, knew none
of the men who mourned her son, then
went back home, childless and bewildered.

How many Nagasakis can one woman bear?

Weak and weeping,
Yoshi's lover gave the old woman a folio with
the aspiring artist's life in it.
He was white, this lover, and full of woe, but
he had a new boyfriend before the full moon.

*   *   *

They say the American navy dove so fast
some sailors lived for days in pockets of air the
size of rooms that shrank as the men
inhaled them. Can these seamen then be said
to have caused their own dying?

Of course, someone knew all the time.
Someone could have stopped it at the
International Date Line, but
the generals were itching for involvement,
as generals generally are, and
a dead son is a premium pretext for
retaliation. Besides, that spanking new A-bomb
needed a target, didn't it?

*   *   *

But where is justice when
some men choose their end
and others burn in a fire
not of their own making, their
shadows branded into concrete,
their tattooed anchors blistered by
flaming oil on boiling water?

Justice is a stray Samoyed.
He happened into Plummer Park one day
and met a young hustler named Stan.
The two are now inseparable since
the kid thinks his pooch will
protect him from
an unwarranted knife between thin ribs,
and who's to say he's wrong?

Justice licks the feet of
Stan's saltier johns, and they don't mind a
bit, as long as there's a leash involved.

*   *   *

Back at the car
you find you've been cited for halting a
motor vehicle in an anti-auto sector.
Yang has swallowed yin whole, but

39

there's no surprise in that:
History is a daisy chain of random death.

The killers all have vanished now. The house
is yours alone. One small kitchen cricket, soft
as a frog or a drowning man's prayer, is
still kicking, but his
chirping is stilled for the good of mankind.

It's Hanukkah, the gentile face on the TV beams,
Festival of Light, the celebration of a
narrow escape they never knew on the
Arizona. You are suffocating under
the weight of symbols.
And night is on you without candles—
you wonder if you are glad Ben will soon
be home—
is on you
without dreams.

Mrs. Edward L. Davis and
Her Son, Livingston Davis
Oil on canvas, 1890
by John Singer Sargent
(American, 1856-1925)

At first I thought the dark aura
around your mother's head
was an optical illusion,
an afterimage in negative
of your white straw sun hat.
On closer examination, I see
it is only paint. She has
a kind enough face but is a
dark and formidable power to
cling to, you in a sailor suit,
maybe ten years old.
Her eyes are rapier steel
fixed above my head.
Your eyes,
a dark brown accusation of
having abandoned you,
track my attempted escape.
You are impatient, but
love the attention, which
Mrs. Edward Davis knows. Mothers
always do.

The tour guide nearby says
you are timid.
I say you were
biding your time.
By 1900, I figure, you were
a heartbreaker, spoiled and
despoiling, by the Great War
a young entrepreneur with a wife
and rasher of children. Did you

long for the boy then as I
long for him now, the one
I was and never was, the me I see
in your eyes, eyes that
call me to pull you
out of the life mapped for you,
out of the canvas into breathing?

Andrew
was no ordinary child,
as he sat on my lap in the
back seat of his dad's
TransAm gunning it out of Alameda
toward his Concord *abuelita*.
I was no
ordinary child either,
his uncle's lover,
him not understanding,
clinging to my beard for
fear of speed and
crying at the airport when I
finally left for good.
Youngest of three,
it was Andrew it was hard to leave,
not the man it was bedlam to love.
I cried on the plane as it
flew over the Grand Canyon at dusk.
The stewardess offered a third
drink free by way of
consolation and asked—
in the way of such things—
if I had any
children.

Man Wearing Laurels
Oil on canvas, 1880
by John Singer Sargent
(American, 1856-1925)

You are the one full of
sex and sadness,
brooding over loss,
bearing the pain of
consequence
tied to your own
appetite, choosing
solitude, not
the ridicule of
company.

Was your body
paid for with
your likeness?
Your portrait,
the guard informs,
is the most valuable
in the gallery, but
you are given no
prominence, little
light. Your dark eye,

new moustache,
simple nipple, and the
forest backdrop make you
every faun I
failed to capture:
David in a dance. But
you are not
dancing, not
playing a pipe or
running in play. You are

sullen, earth-bound boy
on the cusp of man. Your
eyes—almost obscured by
the painter's dark
pigment and intentions—
are cast down
to the ground on
your right
avoiding the sight of
all but cool grass

growing by a stream. Your
parted lips are
the color of raw salmon,
like lust that's
already spent. You appear
hairless (cut off by the un-
generous painter, embarrassed
by his own idolatry, across
the solar plexus), but I...
I imagine hair from

belly on down as
coarse and black as
the eyelashes of
stable horses.
You're a classic, all right,
and my fingers
long to entwine
the moist curls
of your hair
under the vine leaves

an envious boy
placed there, it seems,
to mock you.
A year ago you
swam with friends at

a secret pond, slapping the
water with hands and showing
the sun your skin
in a swan dive
forbidden by elders.

Somehow a care fell across
your face, an emotion
you did not understand. You
became initiate,
are not happy
with what you have become,
with what you foresee.
I could, if you asked me,
hold you in my arms
and warm the cool earth of you—

aloof as nocturnes—
to flowers and smiles. But
no dram of loving will
drain that look of
solitude from your eye
unless you choose.
That is the way of
seclusion. It
seals itself. It
cannot be breached by

another recluse, even
a reckless one who
ventures out
to a public gallery
on a shady afternoon in
search of icons to
adore, oil and
canvas lovers
content to be worshipped
from afar.

The Indian Hunter
Bronze, 1860
by John Quincey Adams Ward
(American, 1830-1910)

In the coolest gallery,
the one with the fewest people,
the bronze boy
stalks:
bent at the waist
in bearskin,
one hand on his bow,
another on this thin-ribbed dog.
He is long-haired and barefoot
with muscles in his back and arms,
veins in his arms and hands,
long toes,
look of sad acceptance
in a serious eye:
a predator
with a conscience. I can
imagine in the autumn night
wrapping my arms around his shoulders and
his shoulders feeling cool,
smooth as the bronze of him against
that wordless thing in me that
hates heat
and trembles a little
each time I
leave a bed.

His Asian lover
For Ben

They have called your eyes slanted,
have likened them to almonds;
I see them a mellow midnight
and in their dawning moonscape
see your love
constant as wisdom and
soft as the velvet down
of reindeer horns.

The silk of the wall scroll,
pale ivory in the long shade
of winter afternoons,
is as smooth as your touch, as delicate,
perfectly wrought: textures and shadows.

And when I am all painted dragon rage
acting the lion and monkey torment
together in myself,
you smile
and calm me in the two syllables of my name:
Your kiss floats on my forehead
like a lotus petal on the placid water
of a scholar's garden.

They have called your skin yellow,
but I do not understand.
To me it is the color of laughter
on a cool and lazy day
together in our bed.
Let the men howl, dogs rage,
let empires fall to ruin like lost ideals,
and your skin to me will be the color of
harbor, safety, succor, home.

I see our love like the endless Wall
of your ancestors,
and we are on it, hand in hand,
climbing each new hill to each new vista,
two background figures on a screen
obscured by flowers.
And of all the vastness of earth,
you are all I see.

Ben and me on Labor Day

When I ask if you want to have brunch tomorrow,
you shrug like you could care less.
"I'm going to the gym," you say, "with
Richie and Jerry." Earlier I say:
"You don't seem to need me for anything anymore."

I meant it as a joke, but you have changed.
"And vice versa," you say/another shrug.
"Does this mean we're both single now?" I ask
but get no answer.

You ask me a question from the kitchen.
Three times you mistake my answer.
"If you want to talk to me, come in here and
talk to my face," I yell in anger like an old
mother out of a bad memory.
You bring me coffee anyway.

"Do you want to go out to dinner tonight?" you ask,
expecting the answer to be no.
"No," I say, "I've already made plans with Kenny."

"Well, there you are," you say. I say:
"If you'd been home today
when you said you'd be home, I wouldn't have made
other plans," and "You didn't eat the croissant I
got you for breakfast."

Well, one more bowl of rice and steamed beef,
frozen vegetables, teriyaki chicken, dish of
yogurt, glass of ice water, one more boring
movie on the television cable later
and you appraise the fit of the sweatpants
you bought me on sale and say:
"I'm going to the gym."

Tomorrow is your birthday.
There is no money
for presents.
There is
no money
period.

You sit in the lounge chair you gave me for Christmas
two years ago,
wearing the T-shirt I brought you from New York in
June. I tip the chair back. You trust me.
I bend over your mouth with my mouth, kiss, and
whisper: "I love you."
"I know," you say, and smile.

How to spend a holiday alone

Your lover will be away on vacation.
It will be hotter than
hell,
hotter than it's ever been in
California.

Sleep late.
Masturbate.
Sit at your desk and catch up on your correspondence.

Take a nap. Shower.
Cut your beard back to nothing.
He will hate it on Monday;
you will hate it already.

Eat lunch out.
Read *The Intimate Journals of Paul Gauguin.*
Visit a bookstore and buy a new collection by
a friend you have loved for a decade.
(The photo on the cover
explains everything.)

Spend the afternoon writing on the floor in front of the
fan.
Write about love and death and the
Fourth of July.

Tire of writing.
Stare at the ceiling.
Stare at the skin-tight sky, rising moon, cheap stars.

Take comfort:
The day is nearly over and
your lover will soon be home,
making sense of solitude.

Sycamore Avenue

The rooms are all empty now,
emptier by far than when we
moved in eight years ago, a
caravan of friends laughing
under boxes of our future.
I've shipped the furniture,
spackled the nail holes where
your picture hung by the door.
I've taken down the shower
curtain with the map of the
world on it and rolled it into
a ball for easier tossing.
Pickett was supposed to come for
the bookcases but didn't, so
I'll leave them here in the
silence. The landlord we have
never seen stopped by to show
the place off to an Orthodox
rabbi. He never said a word
but disapproved furiously of
everything. And, yes,
when I step into that plane
on Tuesday, I will think of
endings, separation, sadness,
and will carry everywhere the
haunting of you in flannel
curled into a chair, of
friends now gone, your
picture by the door.

Leaving L.A.

The starlings are nesting again in the attic,
purple finches under the patio roof tiles.
Merciful, the city has spared me this year
the blooming jasmine that has filled fourteen
Februaries with the full satisfaction of senses.

For one last time this morning the lanky
trashman stopped in his work to wave and
smile. He's strong and dark under his yellow
helmet. I've always meant to ask his name.

And I am on my stripped double bed of
robin's egg blue, waiting for the moving men
to take me away from everything I've hated
and loved. I could not count the friends I
leave behind, so many only ashes now and dust.
In this small crumbling building were Stephan,
Michael and Norris, Tom. Bob died across
the street, Darrin, and John. I'm leaving
a tear or two in the faded brown carpet.

And, yes, I am an eagle—aloft, aloof—
soaring to greater heights in faraway skies,
but I am the mockingbird, too, who lost
track of time and kept the neighbors up
all this last night of my Western sojourn,
blaming the misty moon from midnight to dawn.

And now: the crow is calling from the lemon tree
in Lola's yard; and sounds of moving men, their
hard boots on the derelict unpainted stair.
And for all the achievement the balance sheet
shows, I moved in with a man; I leave alone.

Four

Indiana Gary

At the 'Sixties Café on Santa Monica,
a wheat-white
blue-eyed Gary tells you
the story of his Indiana life:
a farm,
a father who
shot at him when he said
he was gay, a mother who
quoted damnation from The Bible. The usual.

Hair is playing on the VCR;
Jim Morrison's stoned stallion beauty
posters the wall.
Gary wears love beads—
the kind you spent the summer of '69
stringing with Judy in
Rome, New York.

He lives outside West Hollywood
with a cockatiel
and dreams.
You order dessert, hoping to
smell lust brewing with your coffee but
Jonathan walks in
with a friend from
Chicago. Talk turns, as it does,
to death—
and it does.
It does.

The dying makes your head swim—
and you are on the move from
hamburger and ketchup chat of
terminal disease.

You're off like a shot of Scotch
down the parched streets
of Boystown while
Gary fires questions at your back.
You know by now you can't outrun the sprinter death,
but you seek a day's reprieve,
some sanctuary from this deafening angel's
name. You throw yourself at the mercy
of a twink bar
called Rage.

Dressing for work

Today I put on loose-fit, button-fly jeans from the Gap, a jungle-green shirt from Eddie Bauer on Third, and scuffed-up loafers from L.L. Bean (by catalog from Maine). I topped it off with a safari jacket that's equators too big but served me well in Europe, Asia, Africa, and the tropics of L.A.

Saying good-bye to myself in the mirror, I saw I'd pulled on Robert's face like a mask—who I dreamed last night was alive again, and gray—and over that slipped Clark's sweet face, who came the night before and curled into my arms, his nipples harder than ever, and I wore them heavily uptown.

No one on the Broadway local seemed to care, or on the cross-town shuttle. No one said a word on a rush-hour diagonal through Grand Central Station. No one on Lex was the least bit concerned to see a three-faced man on his way to cubicle hell, and two of his faces, at least, already stiff with death.

At the memorial service for
Richard Royal (1949-1990)
For Eve Ensler

You do not want to go but
there are no excuses you can
live with. Eve has asked.
You dress. You go.
You do not let your mind
entertain its alternatives.

Not even splitting your jeans getting into
a cab detains you: This, after all,
is a recurring humiliation, Richard's memorial
a one-shot deal.

Judging the length and quality of
each mourner's reflection
keeps your brain busy.
You want to speak, have nothing to say.
You crave... sex, solace, Italian cookies.
Whatever. You've given up
specificity of need.

Just because you have never met the dead man
does not mean you escape
emotion;
just because he has never met you
does not mean he has not done a
kindness.

You are anxious, bored, engrossed,
indifferent. You want to get on with life.
Who is the innocent boy/man in glasses
whose body climbs in right angles
from the floor—shins to feet,
thighs to knees, and upward in a restless

fidget? Curves are
a café-au-lait child who sits on black
Mommy/white Daddy by turns faster than
a putto's wing; she carries seduction in
a curious eye.

You will not leave early.
You serve your function as it is served
to you, become one with
Mahler's meditations on paradise,
wonder if what you feel is something like
healing, and accept
the lessons of the day:

Death is not an argument.
Life is not the softer way.

Krider at the La Te Da

I.

Krider's got a brain stem disorder of
unspecified (HIV-related)
etiology, which makes him rare but
not unique, he has been told, which pisses
him off, and the thing makes him shake—a lot.
He has good days, when the tremors stop (thanks
to heavy sedation) and today is
one of them. He's on the shaded terrace
of La Te Da for brunch, and he's on a
cane—but he's got the hots for William, our
waiter, a tadpole who keeps pouring that
ice water (so staring into Krider's
eyes he floods the whole patio). Even
Alan's amused. We can all use a laugh.

II.

Last night Cayo Hueso—the name means "key
of bones," not "westernmost key" (in fact the
leftest of the Dry Tortugas)—was ringed
in a roiling lei of clouds that lit the
sky for hours of nonstop lightning. I watched
from their swimming-pooled backyard while Alan
and Krider slept. There is that much life in
Krider's eyes today; you can't fault a guy
for noticing out loud. No one minds. On
bad days Krider sleeps—if he's lucky—and
quivers. That's how it is on Amelia
Street, Old Town, Key West, a visit to a
dear college friend and his lover, halfway
through the second fucking decade of plague.

He lost his lover three times

The first time was in a crowded stadium, where they had gone to see if they could learn to care for the activities other men lived for. (They yawned and ate hot dogs; the other men kept a safe distance). The separation was brief; they laughed all the way home on the express train.

The second was in Paris, near the opera, after an argument that escalated from a difference of opinion (over the relative merits of a taxi and the Metro) into an all-out confrontation over monogamy, fidelity, and a blue-eyed blond named Arn. They found each other later in the Jardin du Luxembourg (where they were, in fact, headed when their contretemps began) and held each other weeping under shade trees.

The third did not feel as much like losing as of being left behind, as his lover slipped further away, deeper into whatever chasm souls collect in when they tire of their bodies. In the place where bonfires had burned, nothing at all remained but a cool blue flame of pale despair.

Important things

Music.
Integrity.
Ketchup.
The Village People and *GQ* (before they went straight).
Air conditioning.
Meryl Streep's husband.
Verbs.
Remembering Marjorie Main.
Remembering the name of the ice-blue parakeet you got
  when you were eight years old: Tweetie-boy? Mozart?
The First Amendment.
Nude boys.
Naked men.
Loving Michael York.
Remembering where you left your car.
35mm film.
London.
Burying the power of parents before we lay them into graves.
Grace under pressure.
Outdoor bookshops and barbecues.
The polar ice cap.
Good excuses.
Sgt. Pepper (yes, still!), Janis Joplin, and Bob Dylan before
  his first album.
Remembering what you said.
Remembering what you meant.
Giving the impression of sanity.
Swearing when you're angry.
Flavored condoms.
Aluminum.
High-density disks and Apple's Mac.
Remembering where you left off.
Remember what you left out.
Having fallen in love in Paris.
Paying attention on the No. 9 train.

Paying no attention to madmen on the streets of Hollywood,
or paying them complete attention.
Paying the rent within ten days of the first of each month.
Capitalizing the J in Jacuzzi whenever it appears in print and
both the P's in Ping-Pong.
The tilt of a boy's hip as he stands with his weight on one foot.
Knowing who you are.
Knowing what infinity feels like and who killed Marilyn
Monroe.
Human immunity.
Blue-bottomed baboons.
Cues, mews, news, and automatic tellers.
Whistling teapots.
Whistler in opalescent shades of gray.
Remembering the names of three Graces, four Horsemen of
the Apocalypse, five Great Lakes, seven Dwarves and
Deadly Sins and Wonders of the Ancient World, all the
plays of Shakespeare, the 50 states in alphabetical
order (and their capitals), and the date on which tomatoes
were first declared nonpoisonous.
Water-based paint.
Red Jell-O.
UNICEF.
CNN.
Protease inhibitors.
Bilingual education and free abortion on demand.
Civil disobedience.
Home Rule for the District of Columbia.
Death to Cardinal O'Connor!
Erotic pleasure, even in this day and age—even if you have
to pay for it.
Positive phototropism.
Oreos.
Logos.
Lightning bugs on the Fourth of July in the potato field at the
edge of the world of Aunt Helen's yard.
Remembering you are no more important than your neighbor,
and no less.

Remembering you are more than the sum of your character defects.

Videocassettes at three for $10.

Three lean boys on a North China beach, eager to pose in bikinis.

Being able to look in the mirror after three days with the flu and not hating yourself for the way you look.

Being able to wake up twice beside the same man without thinking it's just another case of déjà-vu.

Contact.

Contact lenses.

Contact lens insurance.

Friends.

Living friends.

Remembering the names of your friends.

Cemeteries.

Cemeteries of the mind.

Sunset Stripping:
Visiting L.A.
For sweet William Hill

I'm sitting by the pool at the Mondrian
Hotel with Elton John's backup band.
The pigeons are making metallic click-
clicking noises on the aluminum ladder
into the deep end of the aqua dogleg.
The sun is swollen, like a cotton ball
at the back of a night-table drawer.

Barnet's directing two new sitcoms (one
for each of last year's Emmys), but he
starts to cry over his cantaloupe because
his brother-in-law, age 26, died of AIDS
over Labor Day weekend. His wife has
taken her grief indoors, devotes herself to
childrearing and interior decoration. We
decide the mantel is inches too short
(but wide enough) for the dining room.

Betty and Terry throw a party and everyone
shows up,
except for Michael, whose lover died on
Sunday;
Bill's a day out of UCLA, where he's on a
new drug study;
Barry's doing a film on AIDS for Columbia;
HBO killed Gerry's.
Paul was nominated for a National Book Award
but he's got KS now, so
Winston wants a tattoo but he's worried about
Jewish burial.
And everyone loves the would-be mayor—
who woos
the crowd with his smile—and eats caviar
and cassoulet.

Richard thinks I need to take charge of
my life. Oy! He's on disability, so sees
me at home, a tight-assed white condo in
West Hollywood. The advice is all right.
His lips are pale, like Connie Stevens'
on *77 Sunset Strip.* It's a color I've
seen before, as if AZT were a glass of
milk one drank instead of Scotch. If I
move back, and if he lives, he'll see me
again, fees to be donated to the AIDS
support group of my choice.

Rocco and Heidi fly out for the opening
at the Taper, a play about AIDS and angels.
In the dressing room, Joe is exhausted,
wants to wear a sweater, to walk in New York
fall. It's the same dressing room Franklyn
used for that Orton play before he moved
back to Brooklyn and died. The full moon
is swollen, like the Eucharist dissolving
in a plate of indigo wine, or a drop of
grease dissolving in a cold cup of Bold.

My new tattoo itches. But it's a wing,
of sorts, so I assume it just wants me
to fly—and I am in such desperate need
of flying. Of flying and of flight.

Five

Casa de Colombo
Las Palmas, Canary Islands

It was hot as death
behind the 15th-century cathedral
in the broken bottle street
near the pissed-on house
where Columbus might have lived
once upon a time.

The Niña, the Pinta... and Maria, some
say, was no *santa,* but
a stone-age whore on the isle of Gomera,
where Christo hung his hat and
wrapped her in his Latin arms.

Inside the well-plaqued home
an ancient parrot pulls its feathers out
in a courtyard painted with journeys.
But I am

in the plaza
where dogs sleep and
bare-chested boys
(dark and blond,
copper-skinned and
olive-eyed)—

amo, amas—

splash in the fountain of their own youth,
never having known Columbus
or any New World.

71

Portuguese gypsies in the Plaza de España
Madrid

Ask a Spaniard, he'll tell you
the gypsies who live
on the streets of Madrid
are all Portuguese—
begging and stealing,
giving hardworking
Spanish gypsies
a bad name.

But just after dawn in the
Plaza de España—
the sun rising at an obtuse angle to
Don Quixote—
the Portuguese gypsy children nurse;
the women sing
Portuguese gypsy songs.
The Portuguese men strap on the
gypsy day
and smile.
Their blue eyes
dance.
The sun
dances
on Portuguese gypsy hair
the color of
idol worship;
and a Portuguese gypsy youth
tumescent with
the beauty of
Renaissance sainthood
begs forgiveness
for staring.

Self-portrait
at the Musée d'Orsay

In Paris
van Gogh made me weep.
It's there, in the eye: the deep
knowing
that Gauguin—filled with dreams of
paradise—
will leave him unrequited, love still
growing
like apples bursting their skins in high
fall.

He stands wounded, mute at the
news,
oil on his sausage fingers (lifeless and
raw),
brushes dropped at his feet—
an altar offering refused by an absent
deity,
a ring of insubstantial sticks
to batter an innocent victim.

In Paris
van Gogh made me weep,
the paint and pain so deep
blue.
And groaning words, like mad crows,
caw
through wheat fields empty of my lost
you.

End of summer/M. Duras
For Eric Latzky

Running away from an ugly death
I found myself at the sea, face
to face with Marguerite on the beach at Trouville.

Still as dark rock, she wore her
seclusion (a cardigan grown limp
with slow rain). Ancient eyes were crabs in sand.

I wanted to greet her, but words
have tongues. Even a toddling *bon
jour* might have spoiled our mute vow of disunion.

To know her name seemed far too
intrusive; to acknowledge a woman
in debt to solitude the ruin of antique ivory lingerie.

I assume my place beside her. She
glimpses left, I smile; her sapient
gaze (remote, implacable) veers to the envious sea.

And there we stand, two unlit
cigarettes, conjugating love
and wine, refuting death, pondering contemplation.

Gray is the color of Norman fall,
of churches, bunkers, frigid sea,
and Marguerite on the resolute beach at Trouville.

Agua de los angeles

He carried his water
in a plastic bottle
strapped to the frame
of the bicycle he'd pedaled
all the way from the border.
That was Mexican dust
on his sturdy thighs,
Mexican sweat in his
black beard and
Latin love in his winking eye
as he slowed to wave
and drag the toe
of his white leather shoe
along the hard ground,
changing everything he found
in one afternoon
stepping out of a shower.

Desire for breakfast

A brown young man (Latino; surly, of
course; and plugged-in to some yellow-box noise)
sits with an older whiter man (abstract,
given to wistful glances into the
future, and not on a low-fat diet).
Here we all are in the Delta lounge at
LaGuardia waiting for a flight to
Orlando. Though it's just past seven I've:
soaked up Venus—and Jupiter, too—in
the pre-dawn southeastern mid-winter sky;
eaten a bran muffin and banana;
and had a driver who gave himself a
five-dollar tip on my corporate card—
to wit: not a normal start to my day.

The boy's lips—shall we call him Carlos?—move
slowly to the music only he can
hear, his eyes as busy as palm fronds in
a Gulf Coast gale. My mind is saying, Why
not me? The night, of course, will bring Jorge
to my room. He's not a boy, it's true, but
he's available for a price and though
he's hardly waiting my arrival, he's
amenable and expecting my call.
Yes, that's what love has come to in doting
middle age: masturbation and playing
john to an over-eager hustler in
a Disney World lodge. And the mantra runs:
So be it (life is not what I'd have planned).

Carlos, on closer introspection, turns
out to be too young, even for me—he's
not yet shaving (though his eye is famished
for the hunger in my eye)—yes, that's right,
he's just across the aisle, and gay-daddy

turns out to be his grandfather. *¡Verdad!*
This does not diminish desire, the
power of the imagination to
subjugate—or mitigate, at least—the
tepid, undangerously real. But—oh!—
those hands, *las manos de mi Carlos,* which,
now we're aloft, he folds into his lap:
the unwrinkled and unaging unflexed
hands! The unvarnished gleaming of those nails!

At the Atlantic Shores

Here we are, late morning, airing out our
dicks on a dock near the end of Duval.
There's a cruiser anchored off right. The rest
of us cruise lap to lap pool, smooth and slow
(cool low swoop of a Cuban pelican).

There's a man with a ring through a nipple
who's been checking me out, and a kid with
a hoop through his nose who hasn't (of course)
and a dyke with conch-pink areolae
near the ladder into the Atlantic.

There's something about the end of a pier
that draws me to the last plank, where I'll watch
whatever light show nature's horizon
provides, breathless to dive in whatever
lies fifty yards past the visible and

known world. I'm an hour away from a plane,
but this sun and sand get under the tan,
recalling young bodies that were and might
have been (my own included), how hot we
loved once—and how to get it back again.

Oahu
For Joyce M.

The day we walked the sand bar on the
Windward side of Oahu
in the rain,

she recommended Hula's, you know.
the gay bar & lei stand in
Old Waikiki,

where island men meet tourists
and soldiers under the
banyan tree.

She was sweet, Japanese, shy
about her weight, full
of laughter,

and I was drawn to her as to a
rocky place that seemed
a home.

But she was wise, and clearly well
past giving herself to a
homosexual

on vacation from himself and the
life he wasn't having in
New York City.

The day we walked the sand bar in
the rain, I thought I felt
desire,

and knew there was a time I'd
have gladly held a face
like hers

and covered it with sweet hard
kisses in the dark
Pacific night,

and played on coral beaches with
children of rare half-
Asian beauty.

But those days are gone, with a
trill of sadness, like
a slow walk

in the clean soft morning rain
far from Honolulu, on
a natural

sand bar in a shallow sea near
the gusty Windward side
of Oahu.

In flight

It was raining.
The limo came early—well, before six.
There was an inferno on Fourteenth Street.
We took Twenty-third.

He is licking.
He is licking my arms.
He is licking the tattooed muscles of my aching arms.
A cat.

The traffic was light.
There was no sun, not yet.
The dead were still dead and
the Midtown Tunnel empty.

And I am drawing a diagram, a longitudinal section of the Queens Midtown Tunnel in my mind: roadbed inside tube inside rock under the floor of the muddy East River. I give myself a lecture on safety. I think I ought to hold my breath. I have been here a thousand times since childhood. I know there is nothing to fear. But still I am afraid, as always.

A tunnel is a lot like love in this.

He is licking.
He is licking my back.
He is gnawing the fleshy hip at the top of my left thigh.
This hungry cat.

The airport was gray,
the carpet gray and brown.
We waited two hours on the puddled runway
forward from a tower.

And I am thinking that transportation is emotion: Cars are happy/hopeful/loyal; buses sad; trains sad and old; boats are full of freedom; airplanes make me smile—a knowing and bitter smile, a taint of irony subtle as guava—and accept mortality.

A plane is much like Buddha in this.

He is licking my chest.
He is licking the hairs of my chest.
He is sucking the coarse gray hairs of my antique chest.

And I am liking it just fine. I am giving myself a lecture on safety and drawing a diagram in my mind: tongue on skin over muscle over organ, but not near any orifice, not remotely near a fluid of any kind.

Sex is much like painting with sand in this.

Three sensations at once:
1.   Longish hair in a sweep like the memory of touch, whispered;
2.   Tongue—soft, wet, warm; then
3.   Beard stubble as it rasps like a cat whose tongue can strip the flesh off zebras.

(Leopard tongue on the swollen flanks
of an eland wounded in the hunt.)

And I have no fear of him or any real desire. Who I desire—and therefore fear—is a man I know who sits across a room full of my love for him, of which he knows as little as a gene. He speaks, when he speaks, of longing for love, and it eluding him.

Longing is a lot like faith in this.

He is licking, but it is not *you* who licks. It is a third and temporary tongue, a rangy cat from central Ohio who is not named for Dmitry Shostakovich and has, in fact, never heard of music, or you, yet we are three-in-one: you the object of desire; I its incarnation; he the sating medium, the paladin, the means.

I feel the impending explosion like
the hum of an engine out of tune,
a storm implicit in a breeze.

He is licking.
He is licking my groin.
He is lapping the swollen glans.

A cat.

And I am loving you just fine.

A.K.

At school I drank your heat when you knocked on
my dorm door late at night, after stretching
every muscle you own while I sat still
and read about love in a tower. Now
here you are in New York, a respected
dancer and choreographer with a
company of your own and a grant from
the NEA. Dancers half your height call
you Mister and sparkle when they do. Yes,
here you are at the Joyce Theater, twenty
years older and twice your boy size, curling
hair poking from below your casual
collar; and here I am still, lives later,
still eager for the taste of you. Just knock.

There aren't enough poems about fucking

There aren't enough poems about fucking.
There are way more than we need about not
fucking or desperately wanting to
be fucking—usually with someone
dying to be fucking someone else (that's
life). I wanted to write a poem to
balance the scales. I wanted to find new
metaphors for my lips on his lips, my
teeth on his neck. I wanted to put my
mouth on his everywhere—like gold-digging
bishops their word, but something good, you know,
less Colonial, not the odious
Bible lie—as deep in his jungle as
his ignorance of my tongue might be found.

I wanted to convert his skin bite by
bite and baptize the virgin down of him
follicle by follicle with sacred
saliva, to lick the blue veins of his
hard cock (thick as the flooded Amazon
in an aerial photo and hot as
the rain forest equator in July),
to leave on the uncarved walls of his soul
some hieroglyph for the sound a man makes
sliding in and out of a man. Picture,
as I paint him, the hint of fur on his
knotted, concave trunk as it leads your eye
on a swirling trail to the southern bush.
Can you picture? Can you taste—as I can?

I wanted to write a poem about
fucking, but I am with Adrien, and
he is wanting to be fucking someone
else. So he and I stay friendly—with a
sniff of sex around the edges, like a

whiff of gardenia shampoo an hour
after a shower. At the reading I
feel the heat of his neck when I slip my
arm over his boy-narrow shoulders, and
the press of elbows as we touch the same
rest; I can even smell his back—the spine
stretched to vertebrate limits as he leans,
my palm brushing a field of forest green
shirt, fingertips climbing the ridges there.

So this, too, turns out to be a poem
about not fucking—unless you count how
I felt when he said over dinner that
I did *not* fall in love with him, as if
my confession were a simple over-
statement, an exaggeration of lust
in the heat of early acquaintance in
Boston three years ago, hand-in-hand on
icy Newbury Street. That felt rather
like a rape, or penetration at least—
his not having known this thing—the long slow
falling feeling of the small and naked
Indians of Brazil, who never knew
their sweet welcome invited extinction.

TWO POEMS FOR MATT

There are two kinds of days

Some days, everything
goes wrong.

Some days, almost
everything.

On days when
almost everything
goes wrong,
I think of you.

When everything
goes wrong,
I think of you

naked.

In-between

In-between
light and
memory:
you.

In-between
memory and
darkness:
the real

you.

I want to fuck a boy

I want to fuck a boy in the ass who
really likes it, a boy at the height of
his beauty, with that downy hair on those
muscles of theirs, and that skin—you know what
I mean. And those eyes that say yes to life
and to me across a room, *yes,* a boy
who feels a fuck from his asshairs to the
inside dome of his skull, who just folds in
half with a taut ripple of flesh when my
tongue touches his fever-y asshole, who
sucks on my cock while I rim him—*yes*—who
moans with gratitude when I pry him a-
part with my thumbs, who can't wait, who wants me
inside him now, his boy eyes saying *yes.*

I want to fuck a boy (2)

I want to fuck a boy who knows how to
be quiet when it's over, him lying
there in my arms, covered in sweat, spit, and
grease, not talking while my cum is drying
in his dark—yes, *raven*—hair. Who knows how
to be still in my arms after my cock
has been up his ass and my ass has been
in his face and my hands on every part
of him. And then I want to give him one
more kiss on those—yes, *ruby*—lips, soft as—
yes—a girl's. And I want him to look up
in that half light between something finished
and something begun and know I will write
poems now as full of love as those eyes.

I want my dick sucked

I want my dick sucked by a puppy of
a thing while he's having a tattoo on
his left asscheek. I want him naked and
flat on his tight stomach on a leather
table in the back room, and I want the
man with the needle nearly naked, too—
thick, hairy, covered in designs of his
own devising and wearing a leather
vest, his jeans down around his knees and his
dick up the boy's asshole while he works on
the sore soft flesh stretched over clenched muscle,
and maybe he's wearing cuffs. And I am, too.
And we shoot our loads together inside
the kid—and that's how to get a tattoo.

If you could speak

If you could speak, I'd tell you what
to say, a word that murmured
unravels despair.

If you could laugh, I'd shape your mouth
into a cavern where
swans nest.

If you could sing, I'd drink your song
and swallow the candor
of your lyrics.

If you could touch, I'd guide your hand
to a room where a cat is
marking off time.

If you could embrace, I'd melt to skin
and wrap the muscle of your
thick-veined forearm.

If you could kiss, I'd let you plant
your lips in a fertile place
that itches for ice.

If you could love, I'd be the poignant
content of your silence
and never complain.

Interrogation

What are you doing?
                Watching.

What are you watching?
                A house.

What's in the house?
                A memory.

A memory of what?
                A boy. A man.

Who is the boy? The man?
                He has a name.

What is his name?
                He was my life.

You loved him?
                He said I did.

What did it feel like?
                Like an illness. Like falling.

What are you feeling now?
                An emptiness.

What's in the emptiness?
                My childhood.

Who is in your childhood?
                My parents, of course.

You loved them?
                They said I did.

How did it feel?

                    Like sleeping. Like a dream.

What was in the dream?

                    A house.

What are you doing?

                    Watching.

THREE POEMS

For Anthony

The Hudson is angry, white-capped, splashing
on the rocks by the garbage dock. Under
its surface, the river is calm, moving
with the certainty of centuries—as
when Hudson sailed the *Half Moon* into the
full mouth of the unknown waters and sank
into legend: Thunder? The crew at ten
pins. The river was born before the land
I live on was a swamp the lost natives
hunted for food, and will live as long as
it's immune to the human virus. At
one, the phone rings, the moment Anthony's
funeral begins at the Algonquin.
Gray today. There's thunder, but no lightning.

Photo
For J. Clark Henley

Here, at the bottom of a box at the
back of a drawer: a photo of Clark in
a graveyard standing by a stone. It bears
his family's name, as does the style of
shirt he's wearing. Was he sick already
when this was taken? I forget. His wry
eyes look out over the bushy mustache
that left wet traces on my lips. Here, on
the wall near a small kitchen: a Palm Springs
photo of Clark in a frame I bought in
the Catskills. Remember how he kept his
vast collection of children's books in the
upper cabinets in lieu of food? I
remember, Clark. Eight years. I remember.

94

Ramón

Regie tells me he thinks Ramón is dead.
In fact, he knows, but sidles into the
news to soften the blow. Yes, I believe
he passed away, he says on the phone—*passed*—
in August (when Terry died and Steven,
who looked so ashy pale and thin the last
time I held him, his hair a hint of the
thick curls I'd lusted for). So there is no
more kissing Ramón, who slipped from my life
into hospitals and family, a
nephew opening in the Manila
Miss Saigon, the book I lent him a gift,
as it turns out, tendered with guilt and a
longing they've seen before at St. Vincent's.

Six

May Day in the sculpture garden
of the Museum of Modern Art

At fifty, I'm a member of MoMA;
at twenty, I wandered the galleries
more in search of boys than art. Now, I sit
on the wire chairs Bertoia designed
with more on my mind than men or pigment:
how I miss Robert, who taught me Matisse
in salad days (before unjust desserts);
how I'm more Picasso's bloated she goat
now than the Guernica of my lost youth,
Rodin's ancient Balzac—old, aloof—no
longer his Age of Bronze. And there he sits,
a foot away, a sweet-faced boy feeling
a man pulsing in the miraculous
vascularity of muscular arms.

Only connect (God's in the details)

A moment of sunshine, the first spring day.
A woman's purse that resembles a pink
Maltese. Rain in the forecast—sure. Paper
borrowed from a woman who had no time,
pen a gift from a long-dead friend. And then
he enters: Brooke Shields in collegiate drag
(same eyebrows, slight bump on a nose that's still
upturned). Nikes, of course (white), jeans, black T.
Dirty blond and younger than my cousin's
kids who ask me to weddings in suburbs
of New Jersey. (I decline.) His knuckles
are red, as if they've been crying. I want
him, but I'm sick of pointless desire.
Instead, I watch, take notes. Write this poem.

Love/sonnet

Poems are lip prints of the in-between,
of nights already morning; poems fall
into cadence to the left of sleeping
and awake; are what the tree frogs sing when
sunset comes to the Caribbean; are
formal chevrons of migratory geese
under low clouds in the shoulder seasons.
Verse emerges from the tide pools, springs to
rhyme after the hissed reasons of ebbing
waves and before the incoming kiss of
passion. And those of us vain enough to
write them are denizens of the edges,
hugging margins, marshes, perimeters,
inhabiting the border towns of love.

Love/sonnet II

Poems are relics of the unexpressed,
artifacts of secrets too elusive
to find words without paper. Poems are
frames around feelings so thick with acid
shame they etch lines in stone, hard evidence
of crimes committed by the heartbroken
who find their tongues, the florid complexion
of arteries flushed by adrenaline
overflowing the banks of desire,
are skin under the nails of stunned victims.
I write them without hope of pardon: I'll
need their weathered scent—an arrangement of
dried cerulean hydrangeas—in the
years impending of incarceration.

Body of work

They bring me unpublished chap books of their
affection to fill the vast and vacant
bookshelves: the burned-out Alexandria
of my ancient, wonder-starved heart. They are
sweet as potatoes, but these kisslings in
lieu of bedmates are hard as fire to hold
on the tongue. And the rippling back of the
young poet unlocked in my embrace, his
shoulder in my palm, and the heat of his
shoulder on my lifeline long after his
peck good-bye—how do I hold that or shake
it away? how forgive their craving each
other? their craven lack of longing to
devour the oeuvre, the corpus of me?

The wide, wide world

Life without the entitlement of love
is a gray thing even in the tropics.
Yes, there are men enough who for rupees,
pesetas, or rials will bend themselves
an idle hour (longer if they're sweet),
and travel will seem more than anecdotes
echoing through the cathedrals of lost
time, the sudden drenching rain of Hong Kong
or Key West slapping through the royal palms.
But they're only island birds: cockatiel
that nibbles on an earring, shocking blue
macaw beaking a bracelet, sea hawk in
high spiral intent on your drying eyes.
Travel is what you do after love dies.

THREE POEMS

On this rock

Here, in Capernaum, by the ancient
synagogue where Jesus prayed as a youth,
I feel the rain come in from Galilee—
a reminder. Here I stand, my dry hand
on the latest church to arc the home of
Peter (his absent hut an emptiness
at the hub of concentric ruins—stone
parentheses from eons of marking
the spot). His ashes lie in Vatican
state under glass, but his moister part haunts
this grave and chilly place: I am his eyes
now watching the young healer bow his head—
anointed hair a veil—entranced by the
marble arch of his flexed and sandaled foot.

Like Cavafy

It's already dark as the ship sails from
Alexandria en route to Athens
via Istanbul. I am the poet
Constantine, the name of a youngish man
I meet in baths by the Acropolis—
he calls himself Kostas, of course, and is
for hire between cigarettes at the
bar. I am far from home but never from
regret, from lovers not so much lost as
surrendered before the fact. My new worlds
are all shadows, like maps traced from old books.
I sit in cafés near dark mosques catching
Turkish boys by the eye and seek comfort
in the arms of elegiac poems.

Athens, Thanksgiving 1996

A taxi strike has shut the city, but
at dusk I hear the museum's open.
I scuttle off like a frantic widow
to find myself at the dawn of sculpture,
nearly alone. I gasp from sepulchral
kouros to Periclean bolt-tossing
Zeus, my heart leaping past three dimensions,
stopping short in a measured crescent of
marble heads set in a red cove. I... weep:
For here is drowned Antinoüs, in his
recaptured youth, and Hadrian beside
him (adoring), reunited by a
curator's kiss. *Art triumphs over death!*
(but not over mourning or ancient grief).

End of summer: Christopher Street Pier

Something's in flames in New Jersey, as it
so often is (last night it was fire-
works for Labor Day), and now black billows
of smoke head across the Hudson with the
weather (as fine as any this summer).
The men and boys are here (in various
states of exposure), and I am wanting
this one or that in familiar degrees
of futility. I do not harbor
delusions of reciprocity. My
flawed admiration is my exposure
to indifference, ridicule... disgust.
Yet I am tanned by it. My frozen heart
still knows to seek this necessary thaw.

Love and Snow

I.

Love resides in the implied silence of
snow and the softening demarcation
of streets losing hard edges in its mute
accumulation. Love hides out in the
difference between a thing and what you
imagine lies behind a familiar
shape enveloped by snow after a night
of old solitude. Today, the neighbor
couples untrim their holiday trees in
a grid of windows overlooking the
river; I am listening to Mozart
and memories. There's a kindness in snow,
forgiveness I feel on my lips—a rare
baptismal rite, the only kiss I know.

II.

The only kiss I know is gentle. It
loves me back—unlike the men I've squandered
my heart on (blizzards of affection that
melted in the glow of their neglect). One
dusk, I stood waist deep in a field, wet with
longing; I'd been staring into a room
so yellow it might have been the sun. (A
look at the eclipse can damage sight.) I
remember, too, the first lacy flake of
it I ever saw, on the sleeve I wore
my heart on, and a New England boy, now
dead, and this: "Emily Dickinson falls
from the sky in bride-brittle hexagrams."
One kiss, his pulling away forever.

III.

His pulling away forever was a
lesson—a life class in the nude—yes, we'd
gotten that far: naked, London, a kind
of coastal sleet that passes for snow. His
lips were dark and soft as snow banks, nipples
hard under fingertips reluctant to
disturb their radiant symmetry. Our
breath hung in the unheated room, twin fronts
meeting a chilled mass of low pressure. It
was a single taste of him—perfect and
unique in nature, one flake in a fall
I'd never eat again, though I'd watch while
strangers took him hot in their mouths between
icy trucks in a Greenwich Village storm.

IV.

In a Greenwich Village storm, memory
floats down in flakes of increasing size and
spiraling velocity. Ice flows down
the Hudson from its upstate origins.
There was snow on the Greyhound, too, that first
winter vacation away from home, drifts
as high as the Interstate guard rail and
traffic slowed to a standstill. Longmeadow
was a graveyard, white as a century
of pillars and pining. Later, in his
upper room, we took permission from the
needling of snow on a bedside dormer.
When we spoke the secret aloud, it was
whispered—full of wonder, quiet as snow.

V.

Full of wonder, quiet as snow, I watch
my life through a screen—a pleated curtain
frosted to diffuse my nudity. On
the news: New Haven is now shrouded; near
white-out conditions prevail. Oh yes, New
Haven—crawling home drunk, falling one night
into a snow-covered hedge and laughing
so hard I nearly froze. I never felt
a thing. Only the growing distance of
the man in our shared bed, his brown skin a
thing of beauty unlike snow, yet soft, as
delicate, as hard to hold in my "white"
hand without killing it, leaving an ache
as mournful as snow melting in late spring.

VI.

As mournful as snow melting in late spring,
I heard my brother's secret story told:
a thumb of flesh flushed from my mother's womb
(as white and wet—her blood the color of
cardinals shocked by winter, the scarlet
of guilt and fevers). If he'd been a girl,
they'd have called him Rose—for rubella, or
our grandmother resting in peace. He was
bunting to swaddle a family shame.
Snow was inadequate compensation,
always melting, even after I'd carved
an albino zoo I watched disappear
slowly all week long—my ice-clad mammals
dying in the light of a manless moon.

VII.

The light of a manless moon on New York
City shows a Euclidean patchwork
of shadow, geometric graph to plot
the arc of a life on. But the vectors
fail, the only line a curving footprint
where a man went walking with his dog. It's
a heavy snow today, and deep, the way
I longed for Matt or—how many others?
Snow can be deadly, if a soft embrace,
as weightless as a child cradled against
you in a sling for warmth, and as leaden
as a mother's love that never thaws, a
fatal tracery encrusting one more
vulnerable elm in a freezing rain.

VIII.

In a freezing rain, Ben called from L.A.
I was scrubbing the bathroom floor (as deft
a *hausfrau* as a German mother could
desire). Jerry died this morning and
Ben—the ex—was feeling alone. I tried
to comfort, but the words stuck in my throat
with memories: a quiet after sex,
sharing Sunday papers all afternoon.
I took the information, but the black
words on the pale page would not stand still. They
shook like silhouettes of spindly trees on
a snowy hill, a sweep as graceful as
paint thrown on canvas, something I had seen,
a forgotten photo from the 'Fifties.

IX.

A photo from the 'Fifties shows us side
by side: the snowman (charcoal briquettes from
the barbecue for eyes, a carrot nose)
and Little Michael—epileptic son
of the local Mafioso (who would
hang himself years later in a neighbor's
garage). We loved the snow with every inch
of skin and made angels with hands and arms,
wrapping snowsuits around each other. We
were five, but he slid into desire
as easily as cocoa going down
(my cheeks still stung from cold). Wanting him came
later, but he was the first of a line:
small, dark, on fire, melting my resolve.

X.

Melting my resolve to stay strong, the Mass
for the Dead shattered me—an icicle
hitting ground—at the cruelest funeral
of all: Aunt Helen in her prime. There we
all stood in that thin and driving snow, her
grave in a maze of cemeteries in
Queens, as lonely as a keening highland
Celt, ice-blue eyes empty of her love for
me and the occupation of Poland.
Three decades later, Uncle Jack, eighty-
six, is dying one memory at a
time in Florida, none of us left to
him whole: "Are you Brian grown up," he asked
his grandson once, "or as a little boy?"

XI.

As a little boy, I was bundled up
against the deep freeze of a Brooklyn storm
and pulled through its slippery streets on a
sled by my father—a beautiful man
with the untroubled, dazzling smile I would
never have. "You carry a great deal of
sorrow with you," Achim said over herb
tea at Rafaela's just yesterday,
though he barely knows me and will likely
die long before I run out of sadness
(he's been positive eight years now). Today,
the wind is a frenzy, as I let the
sitar raga run, and I want someone
to hold me, and I want back all my dead.

XII.

I want back all my dead, and I want the
living to linger. Last night at Frank's, I
counted six who won't outlive me: Phillip,
Shayne, Andrew, David, Chel, sweet Guy. Well, I
told Achim, letting the spicy scent of
mandarin orange tea steam my glasses,
at least our generation's no longer
a stranger to death, but that's cold comfort.
What I want, as my body starts to wind
its way down to a stop, is a smiling
quiet love who's not afraid of snow, a
lasting, patient love who'll bury me. But
I am a polar bear in a park zoo,
and my long future seems solitary.

XIII.

My long future seems solitary, thanks
to seventeenth-century pioneer
genes that translate to elders older than
ninety. Back then they weathered elements
with broad backs and hardened hearts, and the death
of a newborn was common as mud. They'd
have burned me at the stake, my Puritan
ancestors, in their hoary compounds of
Massachusetts, and all the men I loved,
even those who never knew. Healthy as
the horse that kicked a great-great-uncle in
the head, and killed him, I will trundle on—
forty-eight now, and sinking as slow as
the *Titanic*. I want to die in snow.

XIV.

I want to die in snow and be buried
where snow will fall on my grave; where melting
snow will wash my bones in spring and remind
them with flowers I was happy to have
been in love, to have known passion in the
low solstice, unsated lust and a love
of men and God that went far too often
unrequited. Write this on the rocky
place: "Loved by many; beloved of none.
Eternally alone." But remember
my gratitude for the deep calm of a
northern hillside in winter, and how I
used to say, gladly and at peace, that love
resides in the implied silence of snow.

Acknowledgments

"Kissing Ramón" was first published in *Poetry New York*, no. 5, Winter 1992/Spring 1993.

"Uptown local," "Stroke of midnight" and "Scab's *TV Guide*" were first published in *The Hard Way* by Michael Lassell (A Richard Kasak Book, 1995).

An earlier version of "Bathhouse/Burma/Winston" appeared in *Poems for Lost and Un-lost Boys* by Michael Lassell (Amelia, 1985).

"Dancer(s) with Dick(s) at the 1 Saloon, Key West" was first published in *Eros in Boystown: Contemporary Gay Poems About Sex* ed. by Michael Lassell (Crown Publishers, 1996).

"Personal foibles #2" was first published in *Between the Cacks* ed. by Gavin Geoffrey Dillard (Daedalus, 1997).

"Tongues' vocabulary lesson" was first published in *Central Park*, no. 25, Summer 1996.

"Mrs. Edward L. Davis" and "Photo" were first published in *Global City Review*, Summer 1997.

"Man Wearing Laurels" was first published in *Amelia*, January 1986.

"The Indian Hunter" was first published in *Crab Creek Review*, Winter 1985.

"His Asian lover" was first published in *Frontiers*, December 1983.

"Ben and me on Labor Day" was first published as "Labor Day" in *Fag Rag*, no. 41, Summer 1984.

"Sycamore Avenue" was published as "Leaving the apartment on Sycamore Avenue" in *Bay Windows*, August 1992.

"Indiana Gary" was first published in *West/Word*, no. 8, November 1994.

"Dressing for work" and "At the memorial service for Richard Royal" were first published in *Art & Understanding*, no. 5, September/October 1992.

"Krider at the La Te Da" was first published in the Chester H. Jones Foundation *National Poetry Competition Winners* anthology, 1992.

"He lost his lover three times" and "Important things" were first published in *Northwest Gay and Lesbian Reader*, Vol. 3, no. 3, May/June 1991.

"Sunset Stripping" and "Two poems for Matt" were first published in *Lisp*, no. 1, Summer 1995.

"Casa de Colombo" was first published in *Jacaranda Review*, Vol. 4, no. 2, Spring 1990.

"Agua de los angeles" was first published in *Amelia*, April 1985.

"Oahu" was first published in *Excursus*, Vol. 1, no. 1, Winter 1995/1996.

"I want to fuck a boy," "I want to fuck a boy (2)" and "Love/sonnet II" were first published in *Chiron Review*, no. 50, Spring 1997.

"I want my dick sucked" was first published in *Drummer Hard Core*, Vol. 1, July 1996.

"If you could speak" was first published in *The Colgate Portfolio*, Vol. 3, no. 1, Fall 1990.

"For Anthony" and "Ramón" were first published in *Art & Understanding*, Summer 1997.

"Love/sonnet" was first published in *Byline*, June 1995.

"Body of work" was first published in *Hanging Loose*, no. 68, Spring 1996.

Photograph by Gavin Geoffrey Dillard © 1996 by GAVCO

ABOUT THE AUTHOR

MICHAEL LASSELL was born in New York in 1947. His previous books of poetry include *Poems for Lost and Un-lost Boys* (winner of the first Amelia chapbook award) and *Decade Dance*, a finalist in the Gregory Kolovakos Award Competition for writing about AIDS and winner of a Lambda Literary Award. He is also the author of *The Hard Way*, a collection of poetry, short stories, and essays, and the editor of: *The Name of Love: Classic Gay Love Poems; Eros in Boystown: Contemporary Gay Poems About Sex* (a Lambda Literary Award finalist); and with Lawrence Schimel *Two Hearts Delight: Gay Couples on Their Love.* His work appears in such anthologies as *Gay & Lesbian Poetry in our Time, Flesh and the Word, Men on Men, Hometowns,* and others, as well as in scores of literary magazines and textbooks. His journalism has appeared in such publications as *Out, The Advocate, Dance, Interview,* and *The New York Times.* He holds degrees from Colgate University, California Institute of the Arts, and the Yale School of Drama. He lives in Greenwich Village.

This book was printed in April 1998 by BookCrafters, Chelsea, Michigan, for Painted Leaf Press. The text is set in 11 point Helvetica, and is printed on acid-free paper.